Also by Frederick Seidel

NICE WEATHER

POEMS 1959–2009

EVENING MAN

OOGA-BOOGA

THE COSMOS TRILOGY

BARBADOS

AREA CODE 212

LIFE ON EARTH

THE COSMOS POEMS

GOING FAST

MY TOKYO

THESE DAYS

POEMS, 1959–1979

SUNRISE

FINAL SOLUTIONS

WIDENING INCOME INEQUALITY

Widening Income Inequality

FREDERICK SEIDEL

FARRAR, STRAUS AND GIROUX

NEW YORK

Farrar, Straus and Giroux
18 West 18th Street, New York 10011

Many of these poems originally appeared in the *London
Review of Books*, *The New York Review of Books*, and *The Paris
Review*. One poem was published in *The Spectator*.

Library of Congress Cataloging-in-Publication Data
Names: Seidel, Frederick, 1936–
Title: Widening income inequality : poems / Frederick Seidel.
Description: First edition. | New York : Farrar, Straus and
    Giroux, 2016.
Identifiers: LCCN 2015036374 | ISBN 9780374250843 (hardcover) |
    ISBN 9780374715076 (ebook)
Subjects: BISAC: POETRY / American / General.
Classification: LCC PS3569.E5 A6 2016 | DDC 811/.54—dc23
LC record available at http://lccn.loc.gov/201503637

Designed by Peter A. Andersen

www.fsgbooks.com
www.twitter.com/fsgbooks · www.facebook.com/fsgbooks

1   3   5   7   9   10   8   6   4   2

TO ALAN KRIEGEL

CONTENTS

WIDENING INCOME INEQUALITY

REMEMBERING ELAINE'S

We drank our faces off until the sun arrived,
Night after night, and most of us survived
To waft outside to sunrise on Second Avenue,
And felt a kind of Wordsworth wonderment—the morning new,
The sidewalk fresh as morning dew—and us new, too.

How wonderful to be so magnified.
Every Scotch and soda had been usefully applied.
You were who you weren't till now.
We'd been white Harvard piglets sucking on the whisky sow
And now we'd write a book, without having to know how.

If you didn't get a hangover, that was one kind of bad
And was a sign of something, but if you had
Tranquilizers to protect yourself before you went to work,
Say as a doctor interning at nearby New York Hospital, don't be a jerk,
Take them, take loads of them, and share them, and don't smirk.

We smoked Kools, unfiltered Camels, and papier maïs Gitanes,
The fat ones Belmondo smoked in *Breathless*—and so did Don,
Elaine's original red-haired cokehead maître d'
Who had a beautiful wife, dangerously.
But stay away from the beautiful wife or else catastrophe.

Many distinguished dead were there
At one of the front tables, fragrant talk everywhere.
Plimpton, Mailer, Styron, Bobby Short—fellows, have another drink.
You had to keep drinking or you'd sink.
Smoking fifty cigarettes a day made your squid-ink fingers stink.

Unlucky people born with the alcoholic gene
Were likely to become alcoholics. Life is mean
That way, because others who drank as much or more didn't
Succumb, but just kept on drinking—and didn't
Do cocaine, and didn't get fucked up, and just didn't!

The dead are gone—
Their thousand and one nights vanished into dawn.
Were they nothing but tubs of guts, suitably gowned, waiting around
Till dawn turned into day? *Last round!*
Construction of the new Second Avenue subway enters the ground.

Aldrich once protested to Elaine that his bill for the night was too high.
She showed him his tab was for seventeen Scotches and he started to cry.
(Or was it eighteen?)
We were the scene.
Now the floor has been swept clean.

Everyone's gone.
Elaine and Elaine's have vanished into the dawn.
Elaine the woman, who weighed hundreds of pounds, is floating around—
Her ghost calls out: *Last round!*
Wailing, construction of the new Second Avenue subway pounds the ground.

CITY

Right now, a dog tied up in the street is barking
With the grief of being left,
A dog bereft.
Right now, a car is parking.

The dog emits
Petals of a barking flower and barking flakes of snow
That float upward from the street below
To where another victim sits:

Who listens to the whole city
And the dog honking like a car alarm,
And doesn't mean the dog any harm,
And doesn't feel any pity.

LIFTOFF

On the other side of the street, the buildings sit on smoke,
About to lift off—it's spring!
Cosmonauts and astronauts comfortably in their apartments in armchairs
For the journey to summer.
And actually over here, in here, it's spring also, and I leap out of my study
Window repeatedly, like a loop of film repeating itself,
Leap but I'm yanked back up, leap but yanked back up, on a bungee cord,
Jumped or fell, slipped or pushed, either way repeatedly
Bipolar, particularly since I already knew I had to lose weight, and I start to fly
Back and forth in the canyon between the two sides of Broadway
With all the other pigeons flashing white in the sunlight.
I don't know what I'm talking about as usual, but yes!
I settle on a ledge and, moaning, peer inside the room,
And there you are, old man at my computer, pecking away, cooing spring.

FEBRUARY 30TH

The speckled pigeon standing on the ledge
Outside the window is Jack Kennedy—
Standing on one leg and looking jerkily around
And staring straight into the room at me.

Ask not what your country can do for you—
Ask what you can do for your country.
Here's how.
That wouldn't be the way I'd do it.

I'm afraid you leave me no choice now.
The sequence begins with the grooves
Of the carving board
Filling with roast beef blood.

Everything keeps changing and we want it to,
But don't want anything to change.
The pigeons fly back and forth
And look like they're looking for something.

I went to sleep in Havana,
Turned over on my back in Saigon,
And woke up in Kabul,
With Baghdad as both air conditioner and down comforter.

The speckled pigeon standing on the ledge
Outside the window looks really a bit like me,
Me standing on one leg and looking jerkily around
And looking right into the room at me.

Unshaved men run Iran.
In consequence, Nixon with his five o'clock shadow
Rises from the grave to campaign.
His ghost can't stop—even in broad daylight.

In certain neighborhoods, you hear a victim singing,
Corazón, you're chewing on my heart!
Don't forget to spit the seeds out!
Rat-a-tat. Shot dead in the street.

The pigeon outside on the ledge
Came back from Iraq with PTSD.
It stands there, standing on one leg in speckled camouflage,
Staring in through the window at the VA therapist.

Everything keeps changing and we want it to,
But don't want anything to change. Stet.
Everything keeps changing and we want it to,
But don't want anything to change.

Every day I don't die is February 30th,
And more sex is possible.
Flocks of pigeons are whirling around and flash white
In the sunlight like they know something.

Here's what. Here's who needs to be made up.

Here's who I would do.

The makeup artist is hard at work in the Oval Office.

The fireplace fire is lit with the air-conditioning on full blast.

FRANCE NOW

I slide my swastika into your lubricious Place Clichy.
I like my women horizontal and when they stand up vicious and Vichy.
I want to jackboot rhythmically down your Champs-Élysées
With my behind behind me taking selfies of the Grand Palais.
Look at my arm raised in the razor salute of greeting.
I greet you like a Caesar, *Heil!* for our big meeting.
My open-top Mercedes creeps through the charming, cheering crowd.
I greet you, lovely body of Paris, you who are so proud,
And surtout you French artists and French movie stars who
Are eager to collaborate and would never hide a Jew.

My oh my. How times have changed.
But the fanatics have gotten even more deranged.
Seventy-five years after Hitler toured charming, cheering Paris, Parisians say
They won't give in to terrorist tyranny, and yesterday
Two million people marched arm in arm, hand in hand,
After the latest murderous horror, to take a stand
Against the fascist Nazi Islamist jihadi blasphemous horror and murder.
Absurd is getting absurder.
It's absurd in France to be a Jew
Because someone will want to murder you—

Someone who spreads infidel blood all over the walls and floor like jam—
Someone who, like you, doesn't eat ham.
He/she activates her/his suicide vest.
Children just out of the nest
Wearing a suicide vest
Are the best.
It's alarming
And queer to read Osama bin Laden writing an essay about global warming.
So he was also human, like the ISIS fighters writing
Poems in the manner of the great pre-Islamic odes in the midst of the fighting.

We are the Marseillaise. We are la civilisation française. Make no mistake,
Civilization is at stake.
We are a paper frigate sailing on a burning lake—
Many decks and sails, and white and fancy as a wedding cake.
Listen. The Mu'allaqa of Imru' al-Qays, the *Iliad* of the Arabs, keeps singing
In the desert, "Come, let us weep," while the bells of Notre-Dame keep ringing
With alarm. In one of the Hadith,
Muhammad crowns me with a wreath
But damns me for eternity, Imru' al-Qays, and Labīd as well,
But me especially as the most poetic of poets and their leader into hell.

AT A PARTY

It's her nose. It's ravishing. It's hooked. It's *huge*.
The room storms with the woman's blinding beauty, a deluge.
The face with the nose smiles, then quietly kisses you raw,
Her impossibly lovely profile looking suddenly like a lobster claw.
Kisses you suddenly, completely out of the blue.
It's hard to understand what the face wants you to do.
Kisses you softly, deeply, over and over, and not a word is said.
That's you over there in the middle of your old age asleep in bed
At the top of the World Trade Center Twin Towers, the party's roar
Silenced when lightning opens the floor
And walks into the room and thunder stands there—
With Gauguin's nose—kissing you in the scorched, terrified air.

BEAUTIFUL FABU

Another lovely New York day in May—
The opposite of the overflowing ashtray
Of silent crushed-out cigarettes with their traces of my DNA
Buried long ago in my Pompeii,
My smokestack youth, that I've outlived to enjoy today.

I once was olives waiting on an olive tree,
And I was green waiting to be harvested by me—
But too young, too soon, I started pathetically
Reaching for a cigarette even before I got out of bed, yes, really!
Puffing away on my way to COPD.

The rubble has stopped smoking, Fabu!
You begged me to stop smoking—which I knew, Fabu, I had to do.
The sky was the size of summer, blue-eyed summer-blue,
Tourists window-shopping up and down the avenue,
When the World Trade Center towers fell on you.

MICHAEL C. ROCKEFELLER WING,
METROPOLITAN MUSEUM OF ART

A man with the bulging belly of the rich man of his tribe,
Older than middle-aged, and of course with many wives,
Possibly the tribal chief but possibly a tribal scribe
Who eats and drinks a lot and abundantly thrives,
Walks through Central Park to get to the Met,
And, after, over to Madison, destination Sant' Ambroeus,
A restaurant whose name rhymes with *enjoy us*,
To meet and eat pretty girls before the sun sets, which soon will set.

He walks through Central Park and gets to Fifth,
And then to Madison, destination Sant' Ambroeus,
The patron saint of Milan who rhymes with *joyous*,
Name of a stylish restaurant with a front part about the width
A bulging belly needs to sip an espresso at the bar,
While your typical sleek Milan Italian is the width of a cigar.
Death stands there with its thing sticking out,
Working the espresso machine until it spurts and gives a shout.

How many times have I told you how savage Central Park is.
You have to come while you're alive and visit us.
We'll hold each other, exclaiming, Are we really here! Is it us!
And how beautiful, deep inside the park, when the lights go on, the dark is.
Live captives cooking in the cannibals' boiling pot soar
In the summer breeze musically hushing the trees.
Jakarta, Cairo, Tokyo, Rio, Beijing, London, Accra, Mecca wait on their knees
To be beheaded in their gore.

ROBESPIERRE

Who wouldn't like to have the power to kill
Friends and enemies at will and fill
The jails with people you don't know or know
Only slightly from meeting them a year ago,
Maybe at an AA meeting, where they don't even use last names.
Hi, I'm Fred. Instead of being someone who constantly blames
And complains, why not annihilate?
Why not hate? Why not exterminate? Why not violate
Their rights and their bodies? Tell
The truth. Who wouldn't like to? There's a wishing well in hell
Where every wish is granted.
Decapitation gets decanted.
Suppose you have the chance
To guillotine the executioner after having guillotined everyone else in France?

LE PONT MIRABEAU
(Apollinaire)

Under Eads Bridge over the Mississippi at St. Louis
Flows the Seine
And our past loves.
Do I really have to remember all that again
And remember
Joy came only after so much pain?

Hand in hand, face to face,
Let the belfry softly bong the late hour.
Nights go by. Days go by.
I'm alive. I'm here. I'm in flower.
The days go by. But I'm still here. In full flower.
Let night come. Let the hour chime on the mantel.

Love goes away the way this river flows away.
How violently flowers fade. How awfully slow life is.
How violently a flower fades. How violent our hopes are.
The days pass and the weeks pass.
The past does not return, nor do past loves.
Under the Pont Mirabeau flows the Seine.

Hand in hand, standing face to face,
Under the arch of the bridge our outstretched arms make
Flows our appetite for life away from us downstream,
And our dream
Of getting back our love of life again.
Under the Pont Mirabeau flows the Seine.

PUSSY DAYS

Putting my lenses in, I see No Man's Land in the mirror—
Which makes me think of times in Tokyo so long ago
When, on some subway station platform, in a crowd,
Not finding a single person who spoke English
To ask how I could get to somewhere,
For a panicked several minutes
I experienced near-weightlessness and something quite like bliss.

Once, in India, I crossed a midday plaza—
This was Mumbai, then still called Bombay—
And there were maybe twenty-five thousand people, myself the only white,
And no one in the mob of brown giving me a thought.
I walked invisibly through the Indian indifference.
I crossed across the packed brown Bombay busyness—
A man who wanted to be No Man's Land, free at last.

Now listen, do the right thing, you're a gentleman, be a gentleman.
Empty yourself of meaning
And be a man without ideas.
I went from Bali to Bombay, already sick with something,
From Bombay to Cairo, getting sicker.
Next, on to Tehran, where rooms constantly tilted.
Ah, Shireen, one-night-stand of the Shah, looking as if

She had just stepped out of a swimming pool always.
Many swallow-tailed footmen served much caviar.
Among us in the tent was a spy of the Shah.
I was murmuring hurrah,
Once I learned the guest pretending to be drunk was a spy of the Shah.
Then came the revolution
And Reza Pahlavi fled, and rather soon after came cancer.

And then, poor Shah, came cancer—and looking for an answer.
My doctor in New York was summoned to Mexico City with others
From around the world, but they were not permitted to examine the Shah,
But they could ask him how he was feeling.
Doctors from around the world
Were not allowed to see the Shah undressed
And see the nothingness.

My celebrity GP treated heads of state and me.
One patient was Fiat's Gianni Agnelli, who gave the doctor a Ferrari.
Nothing was the matter with me,
But something is the matter with me.
The Shah needed a splenectomy.
One would eventually be performed in Egypt but too late,
A spleen removal done by a cardiac surgeon, Michael DeBakey the Great.

I, too, took a sickness with me for three years around the world,
But the tropical diseases man at New York Hospital,
After months of tests, couldn't find anything the matter.
It doesn't matter.
I was looking at No Man's Land
Between the trenches and World War I will never end.
Millions are already dead. Hemingway is writing instead.

The tropical diseases man who found nothing the matter
Became the second doctor of mine summoned south of the border.
Tropical Disease Man, by proposing
That the United States, on humanitarian grounds, let the murderer
And torturer into the country for treatment—which then happened—
Helped incite the calamitous Islamist
Takeover of the U.S. embassy.

I long for Hemingway in Paris.
I long for Paris and everywhere else that no longer matters.
I long for the stupid English and the French
And the trenches and the stench.
I long for *A Farewell to Arms* and the sadness as simple as a rainbow,
And rowing across the lake at night with Catherine Barkley, who will die.
My fellow Americans, cry with me for pussy days gone by.

Women sunbathe along the shore of a deep blue sea.
The eyelid of the day blinks on the blue to signify another tropical day.
A mind green as a golf course bakes in the hot sun and from the green
Rises a perfume of luscious and obscene
Pages turning and the woman's legs open and the reader reads the poem.
Something is the matter with me.
I'm too happy.

Pound and Hemingway and Joyce in Paris lassoed
And branded the goddamned English language—cowboys in *Paree*!
Each fellow had his favorite café where he liked to be.
At the top of the stairs leading up to the street from the metro,
French riot police, squatting behind a machine gun on a tripod,
Waiting no doubt for some Algerian, swiveled the gun around to aim at me
On a lovely summer's day in 1960.

I immediately looked behind me to show them you boys don't want me!
I was being stabbed in the stomach, the room was spinning,
And, according to the tests, nothing was the matter.
Tropical Disease Man joked: "Maybe you got bitten by a shark in Bali!"
Twenty little schoolchildren in Connecticut were slaughtered last Friday.
Things happen even in Bali
When you write poetry.

Maybe the world got bitten by a shark.
I'm taking off from Newark Liberty International Airport.
The captain has turned the seatbelt sign off while we're still climbing.
I'm opening the emergency exit door located nearest me
To wing-walk above the Statue of Liberty
And the bountiful chemical factories of New Jersey.
I've reached the altitude of No Man's Land and I'm seeking asylum.

A PROBLEM WITH THE
LANDING GEAR

Cars traveling the other way
On the other side of the double yellow dividing line
Carry people you don't know and never will.
The woman on the other side of the bed reading a book
Is likewise going somewhere else.

You are and you aren't yours.
It's like you're on the other side of the road
From yourself in your car.
You're on the other side of the bed
From her book.

AENEIDOS LIBER QUARTUS

I don't read.
I read Rilke and bleed.
In Dido's cave, they do the deed.
And then she peed and then he peed.

In Dido's cave, they do the deed.
Soon after, Dido will be dead.
If only she had read
Pound's *Pisan Cantos*, her suicide would read like greed and not proceed.

Aeneas retreats from the storm of life to Dido's cave.
He studies in the stacks. He sits there in a carrel.
Ejaculating neon into her from his uncircumcised apparel.
He likes the nether lips over the other lips of this queen shouting she's his slave

No question but the time has come to choose.
I choose labia minora over empire, and a queen shall be my slave.
Is there a country in the world America can't save?
And anyway, isn't every country run by Jews?

Dido indeed is their queen—now weeping hysterically—clinging.
He opens his mouth to speak. He sounds sexy with no voice.
What he'd have said to her, with a voice, is he has no choice.
His laryngitis bashes her—the opposite of singing.

It's an Orpheus for our time stroking the divine strings of his lyre.
It's this new Aeneas strumming his vocal cords into myth in Harvard Yard—
Where to sing without a voice, while technically not impossible, is hard.
He sings, horny for glory, ventriloquizing glory, with rock star fire,

And meantime rakes girls—like leaves—into piles to burn.
That sweet smoke of cremation is how he starts the year fresh each fall.
The founder of Rome will burn books on the steps of Widener and bawl
Like a baby watching the pages suffer and turn.

To Widener Library I have come,
Pursued by my St. Louis demons, and they know Latin.
The walkways glitter like gold. The lawns are smooth as satin.
Dante asks Virgil where the St. Louis fellow's fancy accent came from.

THE POND

A woman asks him please to read her poems.
It would mean everything if he did.
Someone he has never met or even heard of pleads please
Read my poems in a letter that suddenly contains a death threat,
I will kill you soon, poems and death threat together
Inside a handsome quite large envelope
The woman, described as being young and beautiful,
Had brought to the restaurant at the Carlyle Hotel
To be handed to him the next time he was there.
He holds in his hand
An envelope the unusual pale green
Color of a pond,
With the big envelope flap not really sealed.
It opens easily.

AMERICA

Hemingway and Wallace Stevens got in a fight,
Drunken fisticuffs in Paris over who was right.
En garde! Put up your dukes!
Then one of them suddenly pukes.
The moon turned into the sun overnight.

Pound isn't on Mount Rushmore yet.
Support to put Pound there is hard to get.
Add Ezra Pound to Mount Rushmore!
Add his face to the other presidents!
Let South Dakota hear his antique *I'm reciting poetry* voice.

En garde! I don't believe a word the sun is saying.
En garde! I hear the sun announce that it's been praying.
I take my constitutional down Broadway
And pray for the return of all the hostages
And hear the optimistic all-clear siren.

They look like shackled sausages, the hostages.
Please follow us down Broadway.
We're talking to ourselves as if we're homeless,
But actually we're talking on our cell phones you can't see
At first, then you see and it makes sense.

I'm talking to a friend in Santa Fe
And what's he say? What say, friend in Santa Fe?
So many mountains has New Mexico. So many joys.
It don't make sense.
Then it makes sense.

A woman out there home-schools her son.
She breastfeeds him until the boy is four.
They both are happy and seem smart and well.
She's America! Meet you in New York. Meet you at the zoo.
Let's meet at the Met. Carnegie Hall tonight.

She breastfed him until the boy was four but claims,
Untruthfully, it stopped when he was three.
Four is embarrassing!
Four is America!
Land of tit! Land of wampum and Big Chief Big Breasts.

In Santa Fe did Kubla Khan
A stately Astrodome decree.
You enter a private screening room
As big as Topanga Canyon outside
Los Angeles

And rise as high above the Pacific
As the big houses in Malibu do,
Movie star castles the size of mountains,
Where the stars
Feast and rest.

White meat marches to the coast of New Mexico (there is none),
Skies over to Dubai and back in a private jet.
White meat eats dark meat and night. White meat eats light.
The Sultan rides his gorgeously caparisoned elephant toward L.A.
And the only bookshop in sight.

Gentlemen, start your engines!
I don't believe a word the sun is saying.
Drivers, start your engines!
I hear the sun announce that it's been praying.
The hostages have been beheaded.

Mountains of melody rise from a page
Of Pound's *Pisan Cantos*, all-American Pound writing in a steel cage
Made of temporary-airfield landing-strip matting
Turned into an outdoor prison cell
Open to the rain and the blistering Italian sun.

Never mind what he did,
Mountains of melody rise,
For which he is
Battered and bleached and sun-dried and drowned
By Big Chief Big Breasts.

I am no wartime traitor frying without a roof
Under Lord Brother Sun.
Nor am I naked in a cage being rained on.
Nor on a New York City sidewalk homeless, begging in rags,
Shitting poems in my pants.

King Lear, preposterously arrogant and unrepentant and anti-Semitic,
Went to meet the American army at Pisa to surrender.
He walks with me down Broadway on my daily walk,
Reliving his foolishness
With immortal melodious regret—but not humility, not yet.

PATEK PHILIPPE REF. 3842

There was a man
Who had a watch
He couldn't wind.
The crown that capped the winder stem was far too elegant.

The winder knob,
A rose-gold speck—
A dot too fine
For human fingers—was not made for a merely human being.

But there are gods
Who ride the skies
In stick-shift cars
For whom Patek Philippe Genève is their Acropolis.

Their Parthenon
Has Breguet hands
That go around
But every morning must be wound.

There was a man
Who every day
Was Marcel Proust
And made the trip across the park to make the watch shop wind his watch.

CORS DE CHASSE
(Apollinaire)

Our story is noble and tragic
As the face of a tyrant not fun not for everyone
No drama or magic
No detail of what we've done
Can make our love pathetic

And Thomas de Quincey drinking
Opium poison sweet and chaste
Went dreaming to his poor Anne and listened to his own eyelids blinking
Let it pass let it pass because everything will pass and be effaced
I will be back not yet erased

Memories
Are hunting horns whose sound dies in the breeze

THE LITTLE CAR
(Apollinaire)

FOR LORIN STEIN

The 31st of August 1914
I left Deauville just before midnight
In Rouveyre's little car

Counting his chauffeur we were three

We said farewell to an epoch
Furious giants were rising all over Europe
Eagles left their eyries before the sun rose
Voracious fish surfaced from the abyss
The people of the earth rushed to find out who they were
The dead shivered with fear in their dark dwellings

The dogs were barking toward wherever the frontiers were
I carried within me all the battling armies
I felt them rising up in me and felt the countries they were moving through
With the forests and happy villages of Belgium
Francorchamps with the Eau Rouge and the mineral springs
The route invasions always take
Railway lines where those who were going to die
Saluted one last time this colorful life
Deep oceans where monsters were waking
Inside old shipwrecks on the bottom

Heights unimaginable where men fight
Higher than where the eagle flies
Man fights against man up there
Only to fall suddenly like a shooting star
I felt within myself new beings and new capacities
Building and arranging a new universe
A businessman of an unspeakable opulence and a prodigious size
Laid out an extraordinary display of goods
Gigantic shepherds led
Enormous silent flocks pasturing on words
And all the dogs were barking at their heels

I'll never forget that night when none of us said a word

O dark departure with our dying headlights

O tender night before the war

O villages with the rushing blacksmiths called up
Between midnight and one in the morning

Toward Lisieux the very blue

Or else Versailles the golden

And three times we stopped to change a tire that had blown out

And when after having passed the afternoon
Through Fontainebleau
We arrived in Paris

At just the moment the mobilization posters were going up
My pal and I realized
That the little car had taken us to a
New epoch
And though we were fully grown men
We had just been born

PUNTA CANA

I'm floating on the sapphire I am in.
And afterward for hours the smell of chlorine on my skin.

Not for the first time, I find the smell of chlorine on my arm
Makes me ten again and makes me sleepy warm.

Mind you, a whole ocean is nearby,
The waves a golf cart ride away, that I will try

After the lovely swimming pool and lunch. "It's to die!"
My hostess tells me with a sigh,

Meaning the ocean, or life here in general.
Life, in general, is ephemeral,

Though five house servants and two gardeners
Are both softeners and hardeners,

As if we were talking about stools,
As if life were meant for defecation and rich fools

Who wade ashore from the *Santa María*, the *Pinta*, and the *Niña*,
And a servant hands them a delicious, deadly caipirinha.

BOOM AND BOOM AND BOOM

I can tie my shoelaces.
I can do up my buttons.
I can stand on one foot.
I can tie a necktie.
I can tie a bow tie.
The river is rushing downstream.

I stop at the corner and don't cross the street.
I hold up my hand and hold hers to cross.
I enter her body with body thoughts.
The feathery ferns look so soft.
The smell of the air is glistening.
The river is sparkling.

It's a military marching band.
Boom goes the drum.
Clash go the cymbals.
It's the river rushing downstream.
The foam is having a dream,
Tossing and turning in white sheets.

Boom and Boom and Boom
Wants you to enlist.
All the way downtown,
It echoes between the big buildings.
Enlist! Enlist! Enlist!
To fight the Mesopotamians.

A MAN ABOUT TO COME

Dinosaurs just prior to their extinction
Voted Tea Party Republican on the lovely outskirts
Of the orgasm about to flatten the planet.
The radical Tea Party, seeking
Less government and more probity,
Dresses up in the Second Amendment in Iowa
And in Colonial costumes in Kansas, and dumps
Taxable tea in Boston Harbor in Wyoming.
Long live the humane guillotine
That gave France her headless democrats
Casting vote after vote with that awful stare
They got from Robespierre—their Pol Pot—
A Solomon so fair, a man so virtuous, so rare!
A dinosaur with feathers is turning into a bird
Over millions of years, between my legs.
A car alarm in the street beneath
The heaving woman on my bed
Can't stop honking:
Honk. Honk. Honk. Honk.
There is every reason to go on
For the pleasure of the city song,
Every reason to live on and on,
Although a man can prolong—
And a political movement can prolong—

Sheer morning gladness at the brim
For only so long.
A man about to come says so long.

Goodbye. So long.

WINTER DAY, BIRDSONG

At seventy-seven I reached my prime.
But seventy-eight was also absolutely great.
And then came fab seventy-nine and continuing to climb.
I upped my wingbeats to an even higher rate.

From my new altitude, I saw through thinner air.
My age desegregated darkness and light.
And everything was one voluptuous sunlit head of hair
Above a garter-belt-and-stockings woman made of night.

Stars shined above and stars below.
Down there—in the daytime in particular—they shine.
It doesn't matter if it's Chicago or Tokyo.
It doesn't matter if it's white wine or red wine.

In fact, there is no daytime or nighttime, it's all one page.
Crack the throttle wide open, stay on the boil,
Write the poem of merciless persiflage—use your joy mucilage
To wildcat in her tumbleweed for that gusher of oil!

République démocratique du Congo poachers don't care—they'll kill
The last elephants there are there for their tusks.
I require prescription tusk-assist, so to speak, if you will.
My poems are so sexist vicious to avoid being tuskless husks.

I'm looking at a video of my goddess,
One of a library of videos of love I have—
Her performing for the iPad, bursting out of her bodice,
And entering my eyes with some sort of sex salve.

In my astronomy, I lick her cunt
Until the nations say they can't make war no more.
Her orgasm is violunt.
I get the maid to mop the floor.

ANNIE
(Apollinaire)

On the coast of Texas
Between Mobile and Galveston there's
A big garden full of roses
There's a house in the garden
And the house is itself a big rose

A woman walks in the garden
Alone quite often and when I pass
By on the highway lined with lime trees
We look at each other

Because this woman is a Mennonite
Her rosebushes and her clothes don't have buttons
Actually my jacket is missing two buttons
This lady and I observe almost the same rite

AUTUMN LEAVES

Plop the live lobster into boiling water and let it scream.
You both turn red.
Of course you have to eat it dead.
There can be unfertilized roe
That will turn red also, maliciously delicious, called coral.
The colder the ocean waters the lobster came from, the sweeter
The meat boiled in the brain of heat.
The lobster at the end is as incontinent as falling leaves and doesn't know.

It's agony to be turning into something else—
And when you certainly weren't intending to.
This room must be the bedroom, but it smells.
A mouse still alive is standing on the trap, stuck in glue,
Like a man trapped standing on the roof of his submerged car,
Or a woman making love to herself seated in front of a mirror.
Little shrieks from you as you try to get unstuck from you
Becomes a raving hippopotamus that sings and sobs.

The fuel for this ravisher unicycle of a world,
Going faster and faster, ever more horsepower,
Is not the president of the United States anymore.
The man on the roof of the car waves his arms.
The butterfly in love lands on fresh tar, tacky goo.
I'm turning into something I wasn't intending to be—
In agony after the awful metamorphosis
Into a suddenly human being.

It's so fascinating to watch a woman masturbating.
It makes your eyes turn blue.
You watch her doing it for you.
She's watching, too.
You realize it's true.
She's doing it for you.
The man's cell phone is soaked.
He's stuck on top of his submerged SUV yelling into the vast.

The new Swatch wristwatch on my wrist
Handcuffs the suspect for having sexual intercourse
With someone much younger, twisting in the noose.
Let them dangle and twist.
It's agony turning into something else.
Some sort of cockroach that smells slightly rotten
Walks around on hairs for legs and mutters something,
Then puts on a fine suit and goes outside.

Outside it's fall. This is the weather that people like,
Perfect for people who hate the heat.
The sun shines down at a different angle
Through the atmosphere, producing that look, that light.
A first responder is coming with a boat
To rescue the man from the roof of his car, a helicopter lowers a ladder
To the boiling lobster. Let me explain to you something
I've never understood.

BREAKING NEWS

Picture a Native American on her or his reservation
Watching the evening news with tremendous emotion.
The TV anchor tells the Cherokee Nation
That a plane is lost in the Indian Ocean.

The missing Malaysia Airlines jet inspires sweaty hours
Of reporting, with nothing to show or see.
Reporters have to take showers
In shifts between sightings that turn out not to be the missing jet's debris.

Anchors have to wait for the commercial break to piss.
On the other side of the break, the entire network needs to take a breather.
CNN, have you tried *not* reporting the nothingness of this?
BREAKING NEWS! Your car's brake lights aren't working either!

It's news bulimia and it opens your face.
You gorge—then stick your finger down your throat and upchuck the airplane.
The plane and the passengers arrive on the ocean bottom from outer space—
A many-eyed space alien, who looks terrible and insane.

Attention-deficit/hyperactivity disorder cookie-cuts millions of little pills.
Widespread clinical depression requires professional, national medication.
Twenty-four-hour cable news is the talking tit that stills
Your titubation.

MARCH 2012

I had become quite young, the way one does.
Daylight savings time, thank God, was back.
Syria was having a heart attack.
The bee in my bonnet began to buzz.

The city trees were jittery with spring-fever fuzz.
Record high temperatures for March, incredible.
If only you could eat the delicious heat, but it's inedible.
It was incredible how warm and charming it was.

Egypt howled next to a beehive, repeatedly stung.
Egypt swelled up dangerously in anaphylactic shock.
Daylight savings plus Iran plus Iraq added hours to the clock.
It was incredible for Egypt to have lived so long and be so young

And to sing with its one remaining chain-smoking lung
In the tear gas, while the dung fly laid its eggs in the dung.

MAN WITH A MOUTH

American psychiatry goes crazy prescribing
Prescribing
Klonopin and Depakote and Effexor,
Hands them out like idle aspirin in lieu of therapy
To the open mouths of the Three Graces,
DEPRESSION and OBSESSION and MANIA.
The hungry sheep look up and they are fed
Klonopin and Depakote and Effexor.
What lyrical names the drugs have.
Pharmaceutical poets named them.

Mouth can do anything a man can when it opens for pills.
Pharmaceutical mouth moves like an earthworm, pinkly.
It looks for other pink things.
Its hopes are centipedes, each hope with a hundred legs
With a hundred legs.
Mouth can do lots of things the man can do
And some he can't. Or won't. It won't say what.
Mouth-man, play your mouth organ, please, mouth-man.
Mouth has a tongue.
It stands on it and walks.

The psychiatrists don't know what they are doing
With the paint set they have been given,
So they finger-paint
With this drug and that
With this drug and that,

Mix and match, down the hatch,
Klonopin and Depakote and Effexor.
The poor patient goes up and down with the tide.
They stand on their tongue and walk
On sticky hair-thin legs like houseflies
Across the glass of a closed window.

MODEL TRAIN

I

That's that sound.
The whirring sound of a profound
Going round and round
And round a central mound.

II

It circles the department store's Christmas tree all day,
Into and out of a tunnel made of papier-mâché.
It's a passenger train, but something queer,
A freight train caboose brings up the rear.

III

Little lights twinkle in the windows of the model train.
They're neurons firing in a brain.
The brain lights up, stands up,
Sipping hemlock from a stirrup cup.

IV

It's a freight train with a yellow star,
And has a Michelin yellow-star dining car.
Sleeper compartments under sweeping-searchlight guard towers.
Hissing Zyklon B gas showers.

V

A blinding smile is floating in the corridor outside—
Like the ghost left behind by a suicide—
To shine your shoes and every comfort to provide.
The Brotherhood of Sleeping Car Porters is the guide.

VI

A woman summons a smiling porter—
Come here, George—and tips him a quarter.
It was the custom to call all Pullman porters George
Because of George Pullman. *Your real name isn't George, is it, George?*

VII

You're a gorgeous Negro, aren't you, George?
Your gorge is rising, George, I can see your rising gorge.
George, something is rising.
You find me appetizing.

VIII

And he smiles that smile TV dance contestants use
That looks like a boil about to burst. That boil pays his union dues.
The moon is urinating yellow moonlight on Lake Michigan.
It's time to make a wish again.

IX

I wish I may, I wish I might,
Have the wish I wish tonight.
I'm is a streak of time.
I'm is a shooting star of wish-fulfilling slime.

X

I wish white linen in the dining car.
Pretend there are plates of caviar.
Snow furring the freezing air.
The lonely prairie out there.

XI

One sticks it in the other.
One is probably a mother.
They rock back and forth trying to get out of the skin they're in, trying
To get out of the boxcar of sighing, and screaming, and dying.

XII

George's dick is as big as a dogfight.
It cuts through her fog like a fog light.
They're the South and the abolitionist North
Ecstatically flapping back and forth.

XIII

The Pullman porter is the nascent Negro middle class.
Now he sticks it in her ass.
Now he's stepping on the gas.
Who would have thought that this would come to pass?

XIV

Negroes and their leaders led the way
Down the sleeping-car corridor to a brighter American day.
A. Philip Randolph of the Brotherhood of Sleeping Car Porters used to say
To the members: Work will make you free when you get decent pay.

XV

In God's department store at Christmastime are many choo-choos.
Chuff-chuffing to their death are many Jew-Jews.
And then there are the Hutus,
And Tutsis vastly murdering them, producing Hutu boo-hoos.

XVI

Jews arriving at the camp by train
Are each a snowdrop underneath a brain.
Ecstatically flapping back and forth,
They breathe the gas and leave the earth.

THE BIRD ON THE
CROCODILE'S BACK

The man can't stay awake. He falls asleep.
It's noon, it's afternoon, repeatedly he falls in deep,
Seated at his desk or in an armchair, as if to try to write a poem meant
A flash flood of sleep and drowning on Parnassus in his tent,
Or something else equally not good.
The guy's completely gone and sawing wood,
Snoring and snorting—until one snort wakes him—
And where is he? he can't think where he is—which shakes him.

He's upside down and he can see
The parachute he's hanging from is tangled high up in a tree.
He passes out again and drools.
This apparently is one of the Muse's rules.
He hears the pleasant droning of the plane he jumped from flying away,
But he's in his study and it's the same day.
He's in his study now and here's his long-dead dog.
Jimmy, my sweety boy, my Jimmy, come back to me through the fog.

Musa, mihi causas memora . . . you know?
You've seen a baby lift its foot to suck its toe
And then go back to sleep for several years
And then wake up to find a whole nation in tears . . .
Multiple assassinations, black and white, white and black,
Chest covered with medals split open by a national heart attack.
Baby has grown up to be an outrage carrying a weapon.
He's graduated from West Point and found little babies to step on.

Liquid gold streams down the buildings all the way down Broadway
At sunset, after a perfect fall day in May, the sky so blue it made you say
Something had to be God to lead to this
Furious brilliance you wouldn't want to miss
By being dead, for example, or otherwise asleep.
He saw a man once start to weep
But stop himself in time,
Because crying for a certain sort of man is correctly considered a crime.

Look how the sky is turning beautiful black and blue,
Reminding us how the aftermath of pain can be beautiful and true.
The apartment lights before they go out come on.
Hours later it's dawn.
Narcolepsy is supposed to be the subject, but it really isn't the subject, nor
Is the man fleeing from a crime he committed in Ulan Bator.
He didn't cry in the hotel elevator.
He's not the Ulan Bator crying elevator satyr.

That didn't stop the girl with the eating disorder driving the car from crashing.
He comes to after the crash, as usual at his desk, splashing
His face with cold water from the nearby lake,
Though he's already thinking of the next move to make.
He'll move to Rio. He'll move to Napoli. He opens the study door.
He'll move to the little apartment on the second floor.
Every day alive is dawn.
The lights before they go out go on.

THE LOVELY REDHEAD

In the colored section of St. Louis, back
When life was white and black,
I'm skimming the modest rooftops in a stolen black Cadillac,
Which happens to be my father's, and I fly too high,
And wake up in my bed this morning wondering why
I'm an old white man in bed in 2012 in Manhattan
Not next to a lovely redhead whose skin is satin.
Pardon me if I grab the remote before I open my eyes.
They're going to televise
One World Trade Center's rise
While the Empire State Building stands there and practically dies
And the Chrysler Building cries.
The tallest building in the world this morning is Dubai's.
Get over it, guys. Say your goodbyes.

Jabbering jackhammers talk their way into my teeth
As I exit from my dentist's office.
Every street in New York, it seems, is being dug up.
Every day in New York flaps like a stork over streets
Giving birth. Almost every building in Manhattan
Is swaddled with scaffolding while inspectors check
For stuff that might fall off. Incidents
Involving some poor schmuck
On the sidewalk getting smushed lead to city contracts.
Somebody the city likes
Is making big bucks. This is about a smartphone
Surrounded by so much noise
It isn't able to.
No one is getting out of this alive.

No one was celebrating noise
Until the great homosexual American composer John Cage
Discovered the great American sound of road rage,
But with no automobile involvement, and lots of silence.
It's the roar of a subway car
Filled with silent New Yorkers silently snapping their fingers
To the beat coming out of an earbud in one ear,
And music they're hearing that we the audience can't hear.
They rise from their seats all at once and start to dance.
Music turns people into this and
Noise keeps turning into New York.
A drive-by-shooting shout is rap, the rhyming slave-rebellion app.
I sing of noise.
I sing in praise.

The greatest city in the world is like
The prostate in a normally aging man,
Constantly enlarging in some new direction.
The metropolitan prostate
Continues to grow, which to be sure can block the flow.
As soon as a funky neighborhood starts to grow and glow,
The real estate developers move in and really annoy.
They slaughter buildings like livestock.
But good things happen nevertheless.
The Meatpacking District is only the latest.
The Red Rooster restaurant in Harlem is so chic.
Let's sneak a peek.
In summer, there are tables outside.
Blacks and whites, young and old, eat side by side.

This has been the warmest Manhattan
Since temperatures have been recorded,
And the Hudson and the East River continue to rise,
Along with the civilization they are part of—
And the rents in the East Village,
And the number of restaurants.
This island is a toupee
Of towers, floating away.
Don't drown in your rivers, not yet.
Maybe five hundred years from now, not now.
My smartphone works in the noise but can't hear,
But doesn't want to be anywhere but here. What a shock!
Or as they used to mock in the Manhattan D.A.'s Office,
No shit, Sherlock!

A crocodile twenty feet long at least,
With a human leg and foot sticking out of its mouth,
Is basking in the sun in Bryant Park
Right behind the New York Public Library.
I was coming out of the dentist's office on Fifty-fifth near Fifth.
I am always.
I have a call coming in on the other line—
Let me put you on hold.
This is he. I can't hear you.
Inside the nearby Museum of Modern Art (MoMA),
The curators are in an induced coma.
The digestive pleasure a crocodile feels is great.
It makes the eaten person sort of swoon.
It makes for quite an afternoon.

I'd rather talk about the weather.
I'd rather talk about which airlines I prefer.
I'd rather talk about my periodontist and my MacBook Air.
Don't try to talk to me about Guillaume Apollinaire.
Laugh at me if you like, but actually it's sad.
You people who know, know love is brief and being old is bad,
Know tribal wars devour the world, and little children are starving.
Five million orphans in Ethiopia aren't riding
Beautiful Italian racing motorcycles to outrun their problem.
Chemotherapy is as brutal as the cancers it doesn't cure.
Starving children get that look.
I'd rather talk about my London tailor.
I'd rather talk about who makes the lightest luggage with wheels.
The best luggage these days glides along on grease.

Look at me, whizzing through airport security,
A privileged man, a certain age, some hair left,
Taking off my shoes, folding my coat and placing it in a plastic tray,
Computer, wallet, taking my belt off,
Having traveled far and wide, having lived through wars
Without once fighting, having read through libraries
In order to board the flight from here to get
To there. The struggle to leave is futile but
The arrival will be meaningful. Leaving museums behind,
I'm in the security line behind a lovely redhead as she undresses
With me for the X-ray. Let her red hair stand
For everything life is worth.
Her loveliness charms the alarms,
But will the weeds and the wars wilt and wither all around the earth?

I'm on the High Line, goodbye, which in a previous life
Was the elevated railroad track along the Hudson, goodbye,
Brought back to life as a walkway and park to rewrite in.
I'm rewriting my life to make it less accessible, goodbye,
And the parts that rhyme
I'll bury in lime.
In the street below, but a block away,
Diane von Furstenberg's stylish wrap dresses are on display.
Who, five hundred years from now, will care or know
About the Meatpacking District or DVF Studio?
The city is dying and living, farewell,
Along with the civilization it is part of,
And which Diane von Furstenberg is part of the art of,
Once upon a time, long, long ago.

SONG

I want to amputate
My death and live.

I want to be asleep.
That way they can't put me to sleep.

They won't!
I won't.

I want to be alive and be awake.
I want a field block.

Give me the epidural
To remove my Haiti.

SNOWING

Snow is falling on Broadway
Through weeping willows of fog.
I know that my Redeemer liveth
And that there is life on Mars.
This is the State of the Union,
December, twenty thirteen.

Lincoln spoke briefly at Gettysburg earlier this afternoon.
He sat back down so quickly.
Such eloquent restraint, it was almost insolent.
Almost before you saw that he'd got up to speak.
It made me think of Nelson Mandela, who died yesterday,
Beautifully walking out of the Robben Island prison, free.

Such is the power of simplicity.
Such was the power of Robert Kennedy.
Nothing talks power prouder
Than the silence which is louder,
Nothing, unless it's this eloquent restraint.
These men I name were magnanimous and magnificent.

I'm talking about the ability to dominate by not.
Power that sleeps on the floor or on a cot.
Politicians pontificate and strut and plot.
Power that isn't sexual or military.
Power that isn't scary,
Or isn't very.

Contrariwise, nothing talks power prouder
Than a loudmouth NASCAR stock car
Touching fenders at two hundred miles an hour
With a howling pack of four-wheel Tea Partyers
Blasting around the redneck track at Charlotte,
Nothing, unless it's that gaudy harlot, that patriot,

The junior senator from Texas, Mr. Cruz,
Smiling his ghastly Joe McCarthy smarm,
With a broken-open shotgun
Draped over the crook of his arm—
Out with friends shooting pheasant and moderate Republicans.
Congress is singing the Cruz blues. Here's how it goes:

The Tea Party made Liberty
Stand naked on a ladder
So they could look up at her
Emptying her bladder.
Republicans in the House
Opened their mouths under the stream. End of song.

So this time maybe the Democrats have won. So
The Tea Party is a rat being digested by a mouse.
I don't know who you are
Except you always go too far.
I'm open to the not preposterous suggestion that
Nowadays Liberty is hazmat.

What do you really think?
I won't say.
What are you willing to say?
I'll have to think. Affordable Care Act,
Put on your hazmat suit, come on get happy,
You better chase all your cares away.

Whenever I get too happy, at least I know the feds
In Washington, D.C., at least the department heads,
Are there to protect my constitutional right
To split infinitives and to utterly despair,
Schlumping around my apartment at noon still in my underwear,
Trying, on my computer, to sign on to Obamacare.

How luscious is this day today? It is.
And what a precious day today. It was.
Each spoke turns the wheel one spoke closer,
Rotating like a brain
Going down the drain
And starting to forget and the sun begins to set.

Life on Earth in New York is a one-way trip to Mars.
I start to forget the Frick Collection and girls and motorcycles and cars,
And football on TV in ten thousand corner bars.
The veterans returning from Afghanistan rip open their scars.
The men and women returning from Iraq potted in jars
Vote right-wing for gun rights but no more wars.

Abraham Lincoln silently regards the awful battlefield
Where the suffering was sublime.
One has seen the tornado of young men's bodies
In the photographs.
One can hardly bend down to tie one's own shoelaces.
I'm an old man feeding to the shredder his discarded former faces.

Now President Lincoln at Gettysburg rises solemnly to speak.
Now Lincoln sits back down, complete.
I'd never been on the F train and was charmed to find
Dawn dewdrops at the evening rush hour pouring into Brooklyn—
Sweet kids out of whom the movie stars and restaurateurs
They will become had not popped out yet.

By the time we pop out, we're toast. Picture a
Cat being eaten by a mouse. Hot gradually getting cold.
Apparently, more people read books on the F
Than on any other line.
Conceived in Liberty, what are we coming to?
My country, 'tis of thee. We make the pheasants fall.

Bam Bam. Ted Cruz pops out to boast Obamacare is toast.
Bam Bam. Liftoff—toast! Website—toast!
But, once under way, we coast.
All we have to do is live our lives
In space, in the space we have, and not come back.
The sky is black, the stars are trembling.

Hot stars getting old.
I tell my friends from across the aisle
Otherwise we'll shut the government down.
The text Lincoln read
Said
Now we are engaged in a great civil war.

It didn't matter to the honored dead
What he said.
It doesn't matter.
The meaning has no meaning.
Such adorable rhetoric.
So soothing to the palate and the public.

Government of the people, by the people,
For the people—under God—
Fights its way up the endless flights of stairs to the shore
Where an ocean ripples yeses to the black above.
A nation yeses all men are created equal
But above is not looking down.

From the flight deck.
This is the captain speaking.
So-High-Up can't see down so can't see the ground.
But I have a video.
The video makes me giddy, though.
The part when it lovely starts to snow.

When I was young and lovely,
And I was young and cruel,
Snow fell on my father's many,
Many coal yards whilst I in knickers was in school.
Black gold—soft coal—
Was what there was to warm the poor.

Snow fell on the poor and on the rich,
Only snow didn't know which was which.
Snow was falling everywhere in the kingdom.
I prayed to the luminous, numinous
Mountains of anthracite and bituminous
And to the giant trucks.

Standing on the levee,
A boy couldn't see across the snowy Mississippi.
Who knows what evil lurks in the hearts of men?
The Shadow knows!
Knows under the softly falling snow
You are either white or you are Negro.

PSALM

Today is Monday, and I am carbon free.
I don't mean carbon free, I mean sweet land of liberty.
I mean I'm reducing my carbon footprint
As I walk fast past the freezing flowering on Broadway,
The pear trees blowing off steam in white bloom
Despite a sudden cold front chilling the warmth.
I hear airplanes high-fiving and helicopters choppering.
Fire engines bellow and ambulances going through a light go woo woo.
It's an election year, and it's time to declare whom you're for.

I'm for a fine Airedale named Hobbes—
After the philosopher, the dog walker walking him explains—
And I'm for all the other animals I greet on the sidewalk.
Hobbes! I can tell you're a good boy!
Hobbes pauses and looks up at someone
He can tell understands him.
A seven-year-old I'd never met came over to me
At Grandparents Day at my grandson's school
In Brooklyn, and started talking to me as if I were his.

He said both his grandparents were dead.
But don't you have four?
He said his mother was in Paris.
He said his father was buried at sea.
He was Huck Finn, with a gap
Between his two front teeth and in his story, who like Hobbes

Seemed to know whom he was for.
The trees in the center strip of Broadway not yet in bloom
Stick up like antlers above the ones in flower.

There is no excuse for not voting next November
For the clouds or for the stars or the moon,
And last night there was even a bright planet
Next to the moon sliver when I came home drunk.
The pigeons are cooing and moaning and mating
To my disgust down here on earth this Monday.
Today is Monday, and in Florida and endlessly
An unarmed black kid seventeen years old has been shot dead
By a neighborhood watchman, a Latino gentleman.

Who will watch the watchmen?
A huge angel perched on top of a tree in the bright sunlight
Of the Broadway center strip doubles the height of the tree,
And of course looks extraordinary, what an extraordinary sight
On its hind legs like a dinosaur, a monster angel standing on a tree.
I try to imagine a huge winged white of light,
Unmistakably the product of another dimension.
I bend down to tie my shoelaces that have come undone.
I know I will have to look up eventually into your gun.

SONG TO THE MOON

You're born that way—or else you're not.
It's snowing—or else it's hot.
It's like the strangeness, that's also natural,
When it's raining on one side of the street.

I'm back to childhood when I see it weirdly
Raining on only one side of the street. I stare
Because it's rare. How does nature dare!
It's like the first time you hear Bach. You stop and stare—and *hear*!

Everybody watches the weather report
On morning TV when everybody's getting dressed.
You always see something. You never see nothing.
If you don't like what you're wearing, change the channel.

But it's always the same weather, isn't it,
On every channel, and always changing
With the times? I like that
It wasn't raining, and then it was, but the sun was shining at least

On one side of the street for homosexuals
In those not-so-long-ago pre-Stonewall days,
Though it was difficult and even dangerous
And they were often unhappy,

However happy they were.
Samuel Barber at the Curtis Institute
In Philadelphia with Menotti and oh my what gifted fun.
I think of the hard-drinking tough-guy GI Bill fags

I knew in Cambridge, Mass., Harvard
Teachers and fiends with a taste for straights, doing their best on weekends
Not to get caught or killed,
And basically brilliant and frightened and thrilled.

You saw hysterical, theatrical, paranoid men,
Given to hissy fits and Carmen Miranda outfits,
Become calm when a shot was fired,
When it came down to taking off the costume and loving someone.

And Leonard Bernstein was vamping around.
And Aaron Copland
Gave manly kisses. Wasn't Dvořák mildly gay?
Renée Fleming singing Dvořák's dragonfly-winged, ethereal

"Song to the Moon" from his opera *Rusalka*
Is what beauty really is and does.
The water nymph Rusalka, a spirit in a lake,
Broadcasts her sorrow

And longing to the moon
To ask the moon to tell the prince—a mortal man—
That she loves him even if he's queer,
Which she deeply does, whom she'll later kill with a kiss.

GREEN ABSINTHE

FOR JOE LELYVELD AND JANNY SCOTT

'Twas brillig and as if I'd drunk
Green absinthe the night before.
The bed felt like an upper bunk
Ten miles above the bedroom floor.

Maybe it's because I did,
Maybe it's because I do
Drink a bathtub of poison gas each night and kid
Myself I'm still able to.

Hey, something is coming—what's that glow?
It's snow or rain, it's spring.
It's chemical weapons. It's baseball spring training. Whoa!
Mariano Rivera throws a wicked cut fastball—a vicious, delicious thing!

Day after day of gray
For Obama in his second term,
And trying not to be poisoned by the horror in Syria today.
The apple is trying to digest the worm.

Bashar al-Assad (may his tribe increase!)
Awoke one night from a deep dream of peace,
And saw, within the moonlight in his room,
The dead about to lead him to his doom.

The dead in the streets gape and gasp.
The dead smell like chlorine.
Their dead nostrils tried to breathe the asp.
There's a waitress at Café Luxembourg named Maureen.

Maureen, your eyes are green.
Your parents crossbred Ireland with Russia.
The bloody blarney of the Troubles, 'tis obscene, Maureen,
And the Kremlin percussionists, if they can, they'll crush ya.

Yeats walked on the moon and spent the night there.
Back on earth, found his rhetoric and politics and splendor and rage.
Soviet Mandelstam rose like Christ from the nightmare,
Rises from the gulag, sunrise on the page.

Something is coming more than we know how.
More than we know how. An asteroid. Soon.
A world-destroying future is exploding toward us now.
Yangon hurtles toward Rangoon.

Maureen, I think I'd better order while one still can!
I'd like the Syria tartare, please, to start.
Then tender baby baboon from the Taliban in Afghanistan.
Picking a dessert is the hard part.

DON'T BLINK, LIFE!

In 1960 I was twenty-four.
I'm not anymore.

Don't blink, life!
Don't move any part of you until I tell you to.

MONDAY MORNING

The man ejaculates a blood-red rose.
The woman looks on in astonishment.
The sun pours in
As another week replaces another week.

The pill tray divided into days of the week,
Each compartment stamped with the name of a day,
Is full of days and pills on Sundays,
But sand keeps pouring through the hourglass.

25 East 86th, 40 East 83rd—
The man walks past his past.
Blue sky, high clouds, a life.
A man walks down a street.

The doctor laughs and says it is innocuous.
A patient woke him in the middle of the night about
Just this, calling from Las Vegas from a tower suite,
Terrified. Afterward, they laughed.

A man ejaculates a red, red rose.
The sky is blue.
High clouds, blue winter sky.
The sky is blue today.

MAN IN SLICKER

A man is talking to himself again.
He strolls down Broadway in the rain.
He's hidden in a slicker, so he's yellow, obvious.
A rainy day on Broadway looks like Auschwitz, more or less.
He has a fancy accent so he isn't Jewish, is he?

He walks down Piccadilly, more or less.
Not exactly talking to himself, more like quiet shouting.
He's a hotdog wearing yellow mustard spouting
A fancy accent but he isn't English.
In fact, he'd sink England in the North Atlantic with relish.

Down to Eighty-second Street and back each day,
Ten blocks or sometimes more each way.
Like waking from a dream and you realize you're shouting.
But you're happy and you're walking.
I'm quite aware I'm making faces.

I'll look good in my black chalk-stripe suit,
Savile Row astride a red Ducati racer
For a fashion magazine, a fancy joke
Done morbidly, my tongue sticking out like I'm dead.
What if they remove my tongue from my head?

Talking, talking, talking, at my desk, in silence,
Putting my head in the open mouth of my MacBook Air.
Being alive is served to the keyboard raw or rare.
The poem eats anything, doesn't care.
I sing of Obama's graying second-term hair.

It's me—I'm talking to myself again.
I'm walking down to Eighty-second Street
To Barnes & Noble to buy my own book. Blue sky. Summer day.
The Broadway center strip of bushy trees
Is a green fluorescence in the summer breeze.

Let the homeless pick through the trash—
It's a heavenly day in heaven nonetheless!
I find filth to eat and I beg—
And pretend I'm the Shah of Iran.
Anything but I mean *anything* to sing you a Broadway song!

I'm talking on my cell to Galassi on his—
We're lepidoptera fluttering our way to a matinée at the opera.
It's a drastic new *Don Giovanni*.
An absolute swine gloriously sings to his harem of flowers for hours
And asks, Who has a more beautiful name than Mitzi Angel?

We dine, sipping flowers and wine.
Winged butterflies of refinement, each on an assignment.
Galassi's is to inhale Montale and Leopardi
And cross-pollinate the language of the tribe.
Mine's harder to describe.

THE END OF SUMMER

I'm from St. Louis and Budweiser.
I'm from the Seidel Coal and Coke Company and the Mississippi.
I'm from the old streets near Forest Park,
And T. S. Eliot, and the B-movie actress Virginia Mayo.

My mother thought she was the daughter of Helen Traubel,
The vast Wagnerian soprano born in St. Louis,
And thought J. Edgar Hoover, head of the FBI, was probably her father.
I'm from Stan Musial and the Brown Shoe Company.

I remember the brick alleys behind the massive houses.
Palaces and their stables (turned into garages) lined the outside of a long oval.
At each end was a turreted guardhouse above the iron gates.
These were the famous St. Louis private streets.

Imagine freestanding Florentine palazzi on little American plots,
Complete with rusticated masonry and brutal grandeur.
H. H. Richardson, the designer of Harvard's Sever Hall,
Designed one of them, forty-seven rooms in all, hardly small.

Vandeventer Place and Portland Place and Westmoreland.
The Congress Hotel and the Senate Apartments.
Lindbergh's medals were on display nearby on Lindell Boulevard.
I could climb down an embankment and play on the train tracks.

Where demolished Vandeventer Place once stood,
Stone magnificence where Teddy Roosevelt once stayed,
Was not that far from demolished Kiel Opera House, where
Mother took me to hear Traubel with the visiting Metropolitan Opera.

My father had a season box at the outdoor Muny Opera.
My father had a cop he paid who parked our car there.
The 1904 World's Fair was in the magical Forest Park night air.
I hear crickets singing in the dark sweet Missouri heat their insolent despair.

THE BALLAD OF
FERGUSON, MISSOURI

A man unzipping his fly is vulnerable to attack.
Then the zipper got stuck.
An angel flies in the window to unstick it.
A drone was monitoring all this
In real time
And it appears on a monitor on Mars,
Though of course with a relay delay.
One of the monitors at the Mars base drone station
Is carefully considering all your moves for terror output.
But not to worry. Forget about about about it.

The body of the man you were
Has disappeared inside the one you wear.

Reminds me of the story of the man who had nipples
Where his elbows should be and whose skeleton
Was on the outside of his body.
The guy walks into a shop on Madison to buy some clothes
And buys some and walks out wearing them
Wearing them and into the Carlyle bar.
One of the waiters, originally from Algeria of all places,
Recognizes him and says with the strong accent
He has despite many years of living in the United States:
Your usual?

A man has disappeared inside his corpse.
His corpse has disappeared inside a cause.

Reminds me of the video of Robert Kennedy
Announcing to a largely black audience at an outdoor campaign rally
At night in Indianapolis
That Martin Luther King had been shot
And killed and by a white man.
Martin Luther King is dead.

Skin color is the name.
Skin color is the game.
Skin color is to blame for Ferguson, Missouri.

The body of the man you were
Has disappeared inside the one you wear.

I wouldn't want to be a black man in St. Louis County.

A man unzipping his fly is vulnerable to attack.
Then the zipper got stuck.
An angel flies in the window to unstick it.
Here comes light-skinned Billie Holiday, Lady Day, no angel!

A drone was monitoring all this,
Which appears on a monitor on Mars,
Though of course with a relay delay.
One of the monitors at the Mars base drone station
Is carefully considering all your moves for terror output.
But not to worry.
Fuhgeddaboudit.

Reminds me of the story of the man whose smile
Shot out flames and whose skin
Was on the outside of his body.
The guy walks naked into a shop on Madison Avenue to buy some clothes
And buys some and walks out on fire wearing them and goes straight
Across the street in flames to the Carlyle bar.
One of the waiters looks as if he's having a stroke
And raises his hands in Arabic,
Palms in, and murmurs a prayer,
And brings God a glass of humble water.

You can change
From chasing Communists
And chasing Jimmy Hoffa, the mobster union president
Who however supported civil rights,

And change to blessing and being blessed.

Some victims change from a corpse to a cause.
You can change

Reminds me of the video of Robert Kennedy
Announcing to a largely black audience at an outdoor campaign rally
At night in Indianapolis
That Martin Luther King had been shot
And killed and by a white man.
Martin Luther King is dead.

CLAUDIO CASTIGLIONE AND
MASSIMO TAMBURINI

The motorcycle looks somewhat dated but is indisputably an angel.
Like an electric chair before the current goes on.
Like an electric chair before the switch is thrown.
You've eaten your last meal, the priest has left the room.
The motorcycle between your legs is an angel
Revving its desmodromic basso profondo into a scream.
It's Massimo Tamburini's great 1994 Ducati 916 design, the Nine Sixteen!
Massimo's soul in metal, slender as a child,
Glory whose maybe slightly dated beauty sings eternal.
Claudio Castiglione, who owned Cagiva, which owned Ducati, was the Medici
Who underwrote the considerable development cost of this piece of sculpture.
Time, space,
Neither life nor death is the answer.
And of man seeking good,
Doing evil,
Here was an exception.

Speed is the demon. Speed is not!
Speed is the big white breast
That arouses Italian men enough to get them *finally* to leave the nest—
Finally!—though they still love mommy's breast the best.
Up the autostrada we sped,
Claudio behind the wheel,
Chatting when Claudio wasn't taking and making many Massimo calls
On the car's speaker phone—a toy at the time only James Bond had.
On our way to his house on the Italian Riviera,

In a dove-gray, conservative businessman's
Stealth four-door Alfa Romeo sedan
(Claudio also owned a Ferrari P-2),
I glanced over at the speedometer but didn't want to stare,
And saw we were casually going two hundred forty kilometers an hour,
And wide-eyed,
Felt a swoon of pride.

Italy is despicable and ridiculous
And bad and sad
And full of as many flavors of cancer as Leopardi said.
It once was great.
It has cancer of the state.
Is there anything one can accomplish before it is too late?
At Rodrigo in Bologna one can eat bottarga.
One can take a taxi out to the Ducati factory in Borgo Panigale
And say hello to Paolo Ciabatti.
One can reread Montale and remember Aldo Moro.
The tentacles of the octopus ripple like boiling ribbons of pasta
And the suckers attach to buildings and the buildings goose-step
Underwater up and down the Arno.
The semitropical trees on Bellosguardo recite their satanic vows.
The cities are for sale.
Men, seeking good, doing evil, buy them.

Audi, part of the Volkswagen Group,
Through its Italian subsidiary Lamborghini
Has bought tiny, mighty Ducati!
The CEO of Ducati is Claudio Domenicali, brains and huge ears,

Who ran Ducati Corse (the racing department) during the fecund years.
Volkswagen's chairman, the engineer and business magnate Ferdinand Piëch,
The grandson of Ferdinand Porsche,
Has always been a vehement Viennese Ducati enthusiast,
Though these days Ducati Corse keeps losing in MotoGP,
The summit of motorcycle racing and publicity, motorcycling's Formula 1.
Domenicali has to fix that or that will be that.
It costs almost as much as the war in Iraq
For a factory team to compete. And then, on top of that, to lose!
Circuit after circuit falls to the Sunni extremists, Honda and Yamaha,
As they rave their way south toward Baghdad,
Beheading Shia for the sheer bliss of it.

Castiglione and Tamburini have died,
And without them Italy is stupid—
First one and then the other,
Both of course of cancer.
It appears Europe will fail,
The euro and immigration.
Germany's chancellor, Angela Merkel,
Is the only man among them.
Nothing is more beautiful than her political will,
But stupidity and cupidity will probably prevail.
Cancer, cancer, everywhere,
And cocaine sunshine in the Botticelli air.
The exotic Ducati Superleggera crackles
As it warms up to commit parricide.
The power of the new machine
Will devour the 916.

Dante and his friend and mentor Guido Cavalcanti
Are taking the museum tour at the Ducati factory.
Here they can see everything that is beautiful.
The motorcycles are displayed along the walls.
The motorcycles are as beautiful as Merkel's political will.
The visitors are contemplating the spirit of Love.
They might as well be gazing up at night at the stars.
So many motorcycles will lead to great poetry surely.
Guido is instructing Dante in the use of the spoken Tuscan language
And the guidance the love of women gives,
When they are joined by Fellini and behind him Puccini
And behind Puccini Guido's father, Cavalcante de' Cavalcanti.
The motorcycles around them look like birdsong sounds in spring
And everything speaks Italian like a river flows.
There is no sign of any fascists
And we believe in God, even if we are atheists.

MONTAUK

The technician squeezes the bulb to tighten the cuff
To take my blood pressure for a second time today
Next to the professional scales I stood on that showed I weighed enough
Not to float away—
Though I may try to fly.
Exciting to think that above the ceiling is a roof and over it the sky.
I don't know why
It's exciting. It's exciting not to die.

The way I rode my motorcycles was a disgrace.
The Old Montauk Highway ripples violently with little hills
That want to launch you into space.
I did everything I could that kills.
Sometimes in midair
One could see the ocean right over there.
I didn't care
How blue the view. Just grill my tuna caught off Montauk raw to rare.

What's going on?
The tuna's in my mouth now!
(I caught you, life!) Going, going, gone.
North is going south now.
Clear-air turbulence over the Sahara is transparently
Me trampolining up and down the little hills at vicious speed but apparently
I'm better but we'll see
The test results is what the doctor smiling strangely says to me.

DOWN BELOW RIVERSIDE PARK

Down below Riverside Park,
On the river side of the West Side Highway,
I walked along the bicycle path
The Hudson flows past hugely,
Across the way from New Jersey.

And on the other side of the river,
The New Jersey side, full of ugly,
I saw miserable architecture,
I saw the efforts to make something,
I saw somethings that were nothing.

On a stroll near Gracie Mansion
Along the walkway above the East River,
I stayed optimistic till
The neon sign of hope stuttered out in my heart,
The long-lasting stopped smiling.

Why does one write with such gloom and complain
About the joy of being alive?
About wearing a veil of lovely rain
That sweetens an endless summer lawn,
And the air smells always so fresh?

So right now, when I go to a party,
A thing that I do rarely,
I have a twelve-minute rule.
I show up and people are grateful.
People know I don't go to parties.

They see me coming in.
I stay twelve minutes and leave,
But without saying goodbye.
They remember I've been there, they're grateful.
And that's my twelve-minute rule.

Pardon me, her tits are beautifuls,
Tits, her beautifuls,
Side-by-side heated outdoor swimming pools
Steaming away outdoors
In the freezing cold snap of life.

I go for a swim in a mirror.
The mirror opens and drools
Heated swimming pools.
Living a life leaves a trail of slime.
Hurry up, there isn't time.

Means it's seventy years ago
Outside the coal yards at Duncan and Vandeventer.
The trucks are waiting to go out
To feed the poor their coal.
The rich have already eaten their fill.

KARL

IN MEMORY OF KARL MILLER (1931–2014)

The trees are waving their arms around
Like some ridiculous performance of modern dance.
They look like ludicrous John Hollander raving about the excellence
Of late Auden. Stop this nonsense! You're not dancers!
At Ninety-second and Broadway, I'm afraid that's
What it looks like they think they are.

We had droll things to say about everything we liked or didn't.
And weren't we clever and didn't we have fun!
We said everything we had to say
Until the plane ran out of runway,
Took off while it was landing—and you were gone.
Such suffering and sickness and sweet good times!

I see a rainbow above a lawn being watered,
Dragonfly iridescence, hissing sprayer-mist, quiet—
And hear the deafening roar of Niagara Falls—
And smell the dainty rain about to fall.
The shower head is the entire sky!
Jihadi extremists

Will want to behead the shower head
For showering us with delights and letting us do our work.
The plane is about to take off
And at the same time is about to land. Bring back those days
When I complained that your smart-set English (Scottish) thing
Was to mock a friend the minute he left the room!

You've left the room. I will not see my darling dear again,
Which is what I'll call this poem
Written to remember Karl Miller, who has died in London.
I shall not look upon his like again.
I send this teeny, tiny rescue flare into the universe
As things on planet Earth get worse.

FRED SEIDEL

As I wur goin down Threakle Street,
To gerra pound o' treacle.
Who does think I met?
Why, none other than me owd pal Fred Seidel.
He sed, "Is tha goin' t' wakes t'neet?"
Well, I thout a bit,
An' I thout a bit,
An' I sed, "I d'n' mind."
So I went.

Eee, an' it wur a grand wakes,
It wur a grand wakes!
Well, six a clock cum,
And seven a clock cum,
And eight a clock cum.
But no Fred Seidel cum.
So I went whom.

Well, I'd' n' sooner getten me neet shirt on
Wen there wur a reet bangin' at frunt dwur
It wur Fred's sister, an' she sed
Fred wur ill, an' wud I cum t' see im.
Well, I thout a bit,
An' I thout a bit,
An' I sed, "I d'n' mind."
So I went.

Eee an' he wur ill,
Eee he wur reet ill.
He looked at me an' sed,
"If I dee, will tha cum t' me funeral?"
Well, I thout a bit,
An' I thout a bit,
An' I sed, "I d'n' mind."
So I went.

An' it wur a funeral,
It wur a grand funeral,
Thur wur sum what laff'd o'er his grave
And sum wot danced o'er his grave,
But I scriked me eyes out o'er grave
Of me owd pal Fred Seidel.

MORNING AND MELANCHOLIA

Mr. X, a bureaucrat at the UN Secretariat, who, with his wife and child,
Lived in a collapsing Gatsby mansion in Oyster Bay
My wife and I rented half of for that summer, depended for everything
On Shantilal, the sweet houseboy with a shy mustache
Who did everything with a smile:

Plumbing, painting, roof repair, keeping immaculate the long white gravel drive,
Electrician, cook, butler, nanny, gardener, housemaid, *everything*—
Including brilliant, indefatigable badminton—
Everything except the one thing he had been promised
And which had persuaded him to leave his wife and son in India

And come to work for Mr. X in America
For forty dollars a month—
Namely, to learn to drive a car.
He used his bicycle with its basket to shop
For odds and ends the boss or madam suddenly craved.

The one thing Shanti wanted to do,
In his brightly smiling, bright young life and shyness and flame,
Was drive a car.
Every day X parked his car at the station and took the train into Manhattan
To solve the world's problems and leave his own behind.

Me and my fancy friends played badminton for hours,
With Shanti on one team or the other, and my pregnant wife.
How many summer hours we spent swatting the shuttlecock
Back and forth till I finally woke.
I finally told X that, regretfully—

Since he was in other ways such a decent man—
I would have to report him to the Secretariat
So that he would surely lose his job,
If he did not give Shanti a proper salary and driving lessons.
I felt I was finally picking off my scabs so I could bleed, age thirty.

Many years later, I was divorced—
And living in a tiny apartment without hope—
When Shantilal called to say he wanted to come work for me for free.
I explained to him there was no room.
He said he would sleep on the floor.

I took a vow of silence for three months in Paris, age eighteen,
Back in the days when even an ancient waiter was *Garçon!*
I read Étienne Gilson's *Hélöise et Abélard*
And walked past prostitutes late at night.
I read all of Freud in English in Paris in silence.

A man comes up to me and looks at me.
It's my Uncle Maurice and he's scary.
"It's the gossip of St. Louis and you should be ashamed of it.
People are saying you're a dissipate."
And he hands me a highball.

I was about to leave St. Louis and Maurice for Paris and silence.
I was a tadpole in a fishbowl about to be a whale—and breach—and sing!
Someday in Oyster Bay I will save Shantilal!
In a future life, Mr. X will tremble like a leaf!
Someday the houseboy will drive the car!

Meanwhile, small-cell carcinoma loves the brain—
Eats brains with the gusto the French do—does love to eat a brain.
While your brain is being eaten, you're out of breath.
To put it mildly, friend, you're near your death.
I don't know anyone who's had it and I'm glad it wasn't you.

I glance out the window at the apartment building across Broadway
And see someone looking at me from exactly my floor.
A man my age is standing there looking at me.
He appears to be talking on the telephone.
He hangs up, still looking at me, and my phone rings.

SUNSHINE

I had a stroke and I'm not me.
I've been disfigured horribly.
Little did you know that I
Was once the apple of your eye.

Sunshine was your nickname for me.
You don't remember, I can see.
You don't because I'm not the same.
I maybe need another nickname.

I do, I need another name.
I do because I'm not the same.
You're looking at calamity.
You recognize me now? It's me.

I try to speak and when you're near
I see your face is speaking, dear,
And see you're saying something nice.
The asteroid was made of ice.

An asteroid destroyed the planet
Janet lived on. I am Janet.
Even with my wedding ring,
I don't resemble anything.

SUNSET AT SWAN LAKE

My little girl is singing: Ah! Ah! Ah! Ah! I do not understand the mean-
ing of this, but I feel its meaning. She wants to say that everything Ah!
Ah! is not horror but joy.

—NIJINSKY'S *Diary*

Nijinsky wants to be Nijinsky's body double. Nijinsky wants to splash in puddles.
He wants to rip the roof off and let the rain in and Ukraine in and be sane in.
Diaghilev and the rest of our kindergarten class will get soaked.
Windows and windshields—do you understand it's raining!
Headlights on in the daytime in the May warm rain
And lights on sweetly in the darkened living room
Feels like what it feels like staying home,
The music turned down low and cars hissing through the pain.
God asks the mirror: "I don't have the emotional depth other people do, do you?"
He never wanted to, though he wanted to.
God stares into the full-length mirror in the foyer—
The border guard at the checkpoint stares back.
The guard won't let him enter the mirror.
"I only have one feeling and you've hurt my feeling!"

SPRING FEVER

Broadway is the Mississippi, the great river
A mile across under your apartment windows, rushing south
Toward Times Square and New Orleans, pleasure-thrust and shiver.
A mile-wide whirlpool opens its mouth
To gobble yellow cabs speeding uptown
And spit them back spun around to go downtown, in the brown
Fertile springtime waters on either side of the landscaped Broadway center
    strip.
We're heading for Memphis on a paddlewheel steamer
On a going-down-Broadway regression trip
Up the Nile and down the Amazon, route of a dreamer
Feverish with nineteenth-century bare-breasted girls on the Congo
Who will sing you a birdsong with a bongo
About plantation owners planting their seed in a slave after whipping her gory.
Hematospermia, blood in our semen, is our American story.

HIP-HOP

I'm a stallion standing in my stable stall asleep.
Horses do that and their standing sleep is deep.
A woman with a whip waits for me to wake
And fuck until I break.

The doorman of my building tells me she's a fake.
She doesn't ride a horse—it's a stationary bike, for Christ's sake.
She posts up and down on a stationary seat
With her riding crop, looking for meat to beat.

She's not a dyke.
She's not a kike.
What's not to like?
It's not like she's a dyke—

Who would care anyway?
It's not like she's a kike—
Who even talks that way? That's so old-time vile and evil.
She's the kind of woman I used to like to love.

I used to ride girls and motorcycles.
Girls found the sweet-and-sour of being spanked awesome.
Now my teeth are dripping icicles
And my hands are fangs.

I'm old. I hate the old. They look outrageous.
They look like garbage.
And it's contagious.
I've never seen so many old people

On walkers with their helpers, an extraordinary turnout
Even for Upper West Side Broadway, breezeway of the dead.
Old people in wheelchairs pushed by
Nurses on their cell phones is my favorite hatred, along with

Dog walkers who sit on a stoop and don't walk the dogs.
Girls in short shorts
Saunter by on platform heels, misting the air with particles. Vases
Of flowers with glorious asses

Stride brilliantly past the cripples entering City Diner.
Dogs on their leashes are yodeling and will be walked and
Girls with their breasts are ululating
And won't be stalked. I don't believe it for a minute. I believe,

For the old and soiled, it's a rather gory glory.
Fado dado didi dado.
Glory glory glory glory.
Syria's another story.

POLIO DAYS

Why did they send us to summer camp—were they being parental?
Swimming pools—any gathering place—were considered plague central.
Everywhere you went, billboards displayed the smiling faces
March of Dimes kids offered up to go with their metal leg braces.

Imagine being inside an iron lung and having to swallow the rotten truth
That life was going to be one long bad connection inside a telephone booth,
And that you'd been really unlucky and would never walk
Because it had happened before there was vaccine from Jonas Salk.

Truman was in the White House but polio was the president
In the years of the plague, when our American atom bombs were pubescent.
The milkman delivered the milk in unsterilized glass bottles.
Aunt Edna served home-killed fried chicken, wobbling her wattles.

I can't imagine it. Imagine being stuck
Inside an iron lung and not being able to touch your genitals or fuck—
Forever—for the length of your brief stay here on earth,
In a death train's sleeping car's shut-tight upper berth.

Meanwhile, the scenery of cities and countryside flashes past outside.
The tickety-tock of the train on the tracks is the groom and the bride
Making love in your brain rhythmically, or is it the air-pump breathing you?
Breathing is all you will ever do. That isn't true—

You will write symphonies. You will sing *Leaves of Grass*.
You will jump higher than Nijinsky and smirk at him, Kiss my ass!
You will sit down at your desk right now and watch the snow
Falling in a million white pieces, and say hello.

VERSAILLES

The boy is sliding around
On his back on the kitchen floor
Trying to look up fat Leona's skirt—
Thinking he's invisible—
And getting caught.

Striped dress trousers and a black frock coat
Are not out of date
In that world where the kitchen is hot
And the fat cook in her uniform
Is named Leona.

I dreamed
I was the Treaty of Versailles,
Traité de Versailles.
I dreamed women were defeated
And you could make them cry.

But they could make you cry.
But they could make you want to die.
But they could make you apple pie
In the kitchen at Versailles,
And you'll grow up to be the king

Eating hair pie with your eye.
I'm dying for a steak and
For hair pie for my eye.
Leona, I'm looking.
Leona, I'm invisible.

So I set out to write a motivational and indexical
Early-onset Alzheimer's
Poem peephole called "Versailles"
About no underpants—but I decided that I won't,
Because it's rude to point.

MY FIRST WIFE

My first wife, and last!
Nine lives ago, at least.

Forty-five years ago divorced.
Sleek sloop without a mast.

The sleek sloop *Happiness* dismasted,
Broken into sticks on the rocks.

The best wife I have ever had, the only!
One more than I deserved.

Irresistibly, we regret the past,
Like scratching a delicious itch.

I regret my youth a little bit.
A little bit is not a lot

For a guy as big as the sky!
Stop trying to be witty—

And pause unrepentantly to remember
The girls in their summer dresses,

Whose dresses existed to be lifted,
Whose high heels were for walking naked!

And the soft Caribbean in midwinter was true-blue,
On a small white sloop with you,

And Whitney Ellsworth and his then wife, too,
Lovely Whitney, the kindest man I knew.

The race is not to the swift,
Nor the battle to the strong,

But time and chance happeneth to them all,
Forty-five split-second years ago.

TO STOP THE WORLD FROM ENDING

A man sits counting the floor tiles of the bathroom floor,
Counts silently left to right, then right to left, while pressure mounts,
And while, in urgently increasing amounts,
His sphincter speaks up like a kazoo and starts to snore.

Six miles later, working at his desk, the man
Nears Antarctica and the palm-tree beach,
And reaches for a hand to hold, a harbor he can't reach.
The man can't stand lying in the sun to get a tan.

The man can't stand being stretched out on the sand
Trying to turn brown and be attractive.
Because he's otherwise so white and so inactive.
He's otherwise a man of midnight and very grand.

How many times a year does a man have to shave?
How many times a lifetime? It's distressing
To think of all the pressing a pants-crease and undressing
Required to make you look like you know how to behave.

Not only does Baudelaire behave, but, in his chalk-stripe suit, carpeted stairs
Look up at him like looking at a god or royalty.
His rent-stabilized apartment feels a kind of loyalty
To his delusions, and anyway who really cares?

When tooth no. 13 in the upper left quadrant continued to ache,
He wrote a poem saying teeth are not a piece of cake.
He asked his dentist had the two of them made a mistake
Extracting no. 14? How many teeth do a poem make?

Movies and Ducatis and politics and girls
Are the tactics, while counting the tiles, Baudelaire employs.
Back at his desk, he devises toys
Whose bowel movements are a string of pearls.

Lyndon Johnson, unhinged by the unwinnable war in Vietnam, would drag
His secretary of defense right into the bathroom with him.
The commander in chief sat on the toilet, shitting and shouting, and it was
     grim,
Which made Robert McNamara make things up and gag.

Airlines, doctors, concerts, restaurants—and politics and girls—
Are balmy tropical topics which, while counting the tiles, a traveler enjoys.
The King's College Chapel Choir, emitting ethereal noise,
Festoons feces with strands of pearls.

Pigs in shit, in their benevolent electric cars, don't
Stop the world from ending—something only you can do,
Poet of the underneath who
Elevates the reader to the depths, which reversing global warming won't.

The art of sanitation is to rhyme the slime.
Do not pasteurize the woman's sewage. From my bed,
I look up at a sky that might as well be red.
I'm coming in my hand and I'm rhyming I'm.

ME

The fellow talking to himself is me,
Though I don't know it. That's to say, I see
Him every morning shave and comb his hair
And then lose track of him until he starts to care,
Inflating sex dolls out of thin air
In front of his computer, in a battered leather chair
That needs to be thrown out . . . then I lose track
Until he strides along the sidewalk on the attack
With racist, sexist outbursts. What a treat
This guy is, glaring at strangers in the street!
Completely crazy but not at all insane.
He's hot but there's frostbite in his brain.
He's hot but freezing cold, and oh so cool.
He's been called a marvelously elegant ghoul.

But with a torn rotator cuff, even an elegant fawn
Has to go through shoulder seizures to get his jacket on.
He manages spastically. His left shoulder's gone.
It means, in pain, he's drastically awake at dawn.
A friend of his with pancreatic cancer, who will die,
Is not in pain so far, and she will try
To palliate her death, is what her life is now.
The fellow's thinking to himself, Yes but how?
Riding a motorcycle very fast is one way to.
The moon and stars rapidly enter you
While you excrete the sun. You ride across the earth

Looking for a place to lay the eggs of your rebirth.
The eggs crack open and out comes everyone.
The chicks chirp, and it's begun, and it's fun.

You keep on writing till you write yourself away,
And even after—when you're nothing—you still stay.
The eggs crack open and out comes everyone.
The chicks chirp, the poems speak—and it's again begun!
Speaking of someone else for a change, not me,
There was that time in Stockholm when, so strangely,
Outside a restaurant, in blinding daylight, a tiny bird
Circled forever around us and then without a word
Lightly, lightly landed on my head and settled there
And you burst into tears. I was unaware
That ten years before the same thing had happened just
After your young daughter died and now it must
Have been Maria come back from the dead a second time to speak
And receive the recognition we all seek.

POET AT SEVENTY-EIGHT

FOR MICHAEL LEONARD

You wonder who in the world are the people who actually use stool cards.
They're the very same scum who sell drugs to little kids in school yards.
The doctor tells you do this, do that.
Simon says screw this, Simon says you shat
And that's enough,
And for heaven's sake don't give in to their guff.
Once upon a time, a man had blood in his stool because he was pregnant.
Poetry and fantasy in those days were regnant.
Stool cards pinch a smidge from a fecal specimen—you wanted to know—
And if there's blood it will show in the sensitive paper window.
There ought to be a rule
That you have to think of Einstein when you examine your stool
In the toilet bowl, and then you have to go out and vote
Because we live in a democracy and you can't simply float
Your life away playing with rubber duckies. Sure, they're cute bright yellow,
But you're a voter and you're a serious fellow.
Tigers facing extinction don't use stool cards.
They're confined in their stripes to prison yards watched by prison guards.
They rhyme and they roar—dyed-in-the-wool, blood-in-the-stool stool bards!
They drool, thinking of meat they can't eat. They're drool hards!
They're the very same scum who sell drugs to little kids in school yards.
They shouldn't but they do,
And, if you could, so would you,
Sell the rap crap you write to innocents standing around in bleak concrete,

No different from selling drugs on the street, corruption complete,
And don't forget to vote.
That's what the tiger wrote.
You're a tiger and the rubber ducks you play with are bright yellow,
And you're a bright fellow.
Pigeons flashing white in the sunlight
Are flashing back and forth in either panic or sunshine delight.
Outside the window is the world
Of glory unfurled.

TO PHILIP ROTH,
FOR HIS EIGHTIETH

I'm Mussolini,
And the woman spread out on my enormous *Duce* desk looks teeny.
The desk becomes an altar, sacred.
The woman's naked.

I call the woman teeny only because I need the rhyme.
The shock of naked looks huge on top of a desktop and the slime.
Duce! Duce! Duce! is what girls get wet with.
This one's perhaps the wettest one's ever met with.

Mussolini often did this,
Boots on, on the desk he worked at.
I'm sitting in my desk chair staring at *IT* and Oh she likes that.
She likes me staring at her box office.

Isn't everything theater? That's what's real.
I've got the face of an anteater
That sticks out like a penis to eat a meal.
I'm a chinless cheater wife-beater attending the theater.

It has to be someone else's wife.
Of course!
I live alone with my life.
One divorce for me was enough divorce.

I think of the late Joe Fox and his notion
That he couldn't sleep without a woman in his bed.
He also loved the ocean
And published Philip Roth when filthy Philip first got read.

When pre-spring March snow soft-focuses the city,
And the trees express their branches like lungs showing off their bronchi,
And the lined-up carriage horses stomp their hooves and whiten patiently,
I stay chained to my desk, honky honking honky.

WHAT A DAY

The blue sky is Sunni.
The white clouds are Shia.
The sun is happy.
The shops are crowded.

The planet is healthy.
The oceans are healthy.
The oceans have recovered.
The economy has recovered.

Long ago, when I could sleep the night through
Without having to get up to pee,
I'd wake at a very early hour in the French countryside,
In my bed in New York, with sweet birds singing *oui-oui*.

Those days of having a car in the city
And looking for places to park,
And drinking martinis at lunch,
When New York was a lark

Of drink and anger and glamour,
Are gone now—and New York is so much better!
And, incredibly, nothing has got worse!
The rapturous casket does an entrechat leaping out of the hearse

Into the blue sky over Broadway—which is Sunni—
And the featherbed summer clouds—which are Shia.
The homeless may be loony, filthy, out-of-tuney,
But the shops are crowded.

WIDENING INCOME INEQUALITY

I live a life of appetite and, yes, that's right,
I live a life of privilege in New York,
Eating buttered toast in bed with cunty fingers on Sunday morning.
Say that again?
I have a rule—
I never give to beggars in the street who hold their hands out.

I woke up this morning in my air-conditioning.
At the end of my legs were my feet.
Foot and foot stretched out outside the duvet looking for me!
Get up. Giddyup. Get going.
My feet were there on the far side of my legs.
Get up. Giddyup. Get going.

I don't really think I am going to.
Obama is doing just fine.
I don't think I'm going to.
Get up. Giddyup. Get going.
I can see out the window it isn't raining.
So much for the endless forecasts, always wrong.

The poor are poorer than they ever were.
The rich are richer than the poor.
Is it true about the poor?
It's always possible to be amusing.
I saw a rat down in the subway.
So what if you saw a rat.

I admire the poor profusely.
I want their autograph.
They make me shy.
I keep my distance.
I'm getting to the bottom of the island.
Lower Broadway comes to a boil and City Hall is boiling.

I'm half asleep but I'm awake.
At the other end of me are my feet
In shoes of considerable sophistication
Walking down Broadway in the heat.
I'm half asleep in the heat.
I'm, so to speak, wearing a hat.

I'm no Saint Francis.
I'm in one of my trances.
When I look in a mirror,
There's an old man in a trance.
There's a Gobi Desert,
And that's poetry, or rather rhetoric.

You see what happens if you don't make sense?
It only makes sense to not.
You feel the flicker of a hummingbird
It takes a second to find.
You hear a whirr.
It's here. It's there. It hovers, begging, hand out.

One lives a life of appetite and, yes,
Lives a life of privilege in New York.
So many wretched refuse with their hands out.
Help me please get something to eat.
I'm a pope in a pulpit of air-conditioned humility
And widening income inequality, eating mostly pussy.

A lady-in-waiting at the imperial court
Flutters her fan in the Heian (Kyoto) heat.
How delicately she does it.
You can't see
How you want to live?
She perspires only a bit.

Outside the Department of Motor Vehicles palace, Francis of Assisi
Is eating garbage with the homeless
And writing a poem to God,
And to our lord Brother Sun.
Never mind that the sun is dangerously hot
Out on the sidewalk.

Open your arms like a fresh pack of cards
And shuffle the deck.
Now open your heart.
Now open your art.
Now get down on your knees in the street
And eat.